LEAFLETS

LEAFLETS

POEMS

1965-1968

Adrienne Rich

W · W · NORTON & COMPANY · INC ·

NEW YORK

Some of these poems have appeared in the following periodicals:

"Night Watch," "Charleston in the 1860's," and Six *ghazals* in *The Nation*; "The Demon Lover" in *The New York Review of Books*; "For a Russian Poet," "Night in the Kitchen," "5:30 A.M.," "The Break," and "Implosions" in *Poetry*; "In The Evening," "Continuum," "The Observer," and "Gabriel" in *The Quarterly Review of Literature*; "On Edges" and Four *ghazals* in *The New Republic*.

SBN   393   04200   6   Cloth Edition

SBN   393   04191   3   Paper Edition

FOR *Rose Marie* AND *Hayden Carruth*

CONTENTS

7

PART THREE: GHAZALS (HOMAGE TO GHALIB)

PART ONE
NIGHT WATCH

◆ ORION

Far back when I went zig-zagging
through tamarack pastures
you were my genius, you
my cast-iron Viking, my helmed
lion-heart king in prison.
Years later now you're young

my fierce half-brother, staring
down from that simplified west
your breast open, your belt dragged down
by an oldfashioned thing, a sword
the last bravado you won't give over
though it weighs you down as you stride

and the stars in it are dim
and maybe have stopped burning.
But you burn, and I know it;
as I throw back my head to take you in
an old transfusion happens again:
divine astronomy is nothing to it.

Indoors I bruise and blunder,
break faith, leave ill enough
alone, a dead child born in the dark.
Night cracks up over the chimney,
pieces of time, frozen geodes
come showering down in the grate.

A man reaches behind my eyes
and finds them empty
a woman's head turns away
from my head in the mirror
children are dying my death
and eating crumbs of my life.

Pity is not your forte.
Calmly you ache up there
pinned aloft in your crow's nest,
my speechless pirate!
You take it all for granted
and when I look you back

it's with a starlike eye
shooting its cold and egotistical spear
where it can do least damage.
Breathe deep! No hurt, no pardon
out here in the cold with you
you with your back to the wall.

1965

◈ HOLDING OUT

The hunters' shack will do,
abandoned, untended, unmended
in its cul-de-sac of alders.
Inside, who knows what
hovel-keeping essentials—
a grey saucepan, a broom, a clock
stopped at last autumn's last hour—
all or any, what matter.

The point is, it's a shelter,
a place more in- than outside.
From that we could begin.
And the wind is surely rising,
snow is in the alders.
Maybe the stovepipe is sound,
maybe the smoke will do us in
at first—no matter.

Late afternoons the ice
squeaks underfoot like mica,
and when the sun drops red and moon-
faced back of the gun-colored firs,
the best intentions are none too good.
Then we have to make a go of it
in the smoke with the dark outside
and our love in our boots at first—
no matter.

1965

◆ FLESH AND BLOOD
  for C.

A cracked walk in the garden,
white violets choking in the ivy,
then, O then . . .
Everyone else I've had to tell how it was,
only not you.

Nerve-white, the cloud came walking
over the crests of tallest trees.
Doors slammed. We
fell asleep, hot Sundays, in our slips,
two mad little goldfish

fluttering in a drying pond.
Nobody's seen the trouble I've seen
but you.
Our jokes are funnier for that
you'd say
and, Lord, it's true.

1965

IN THE EVENING

Three hours chain-smoking words
and you move on. We stand in the porch,
two archaic figures: a woman and a man.

The old masters, the old sources,
haven't a clue what we're about,
shivering here in the half-dark 'sixties.

Our minds hover in a famous impasse
and cling together. Your hand
grips mine like a railing on an icy night.

The wall of the house is bleeding. Firethorn!
The moon, cracked every which-way,
pushes steadily on.

1966

MISSING THE POINT

There it was, all along,
twisted up in that green vine-thread,
in the skeins of marble,
on the table behind them—those two!
white-faced and undeterred—
everything doubled: forks,
brown glass tumblers, echoing plates,
two crumbled portions of bread.

That was the point that was missed
when they left the room with its wavy light
and pale curtains blowing
and guessed the banquet was over, the picnic
under the leaves was over,
when haggling faces pushed in for a look
and the gingerbread village shrieked outside:
Who's in the wrong? Who's in the wrong?

1966

CITY

from the Dutch of Gerrit Achterberg

Maybe you spoke to someone
and on that hour your face
printed itself for good.
Where is that man? I need
to find him before he dies
and see you drift across his retina.

You have played with children.
They will run up to me
whenever you
come home free in their dreams.

Houses, realized by you,
slumber in that web.

Streets suppose you
in other streets, and call:
Evening papers . . .
Strawberries . . .

The city has changed hands;
the plan you gave it, fallen through.

DWINGELO

from the Dutch of Gerrit Achterberg

In the never, still arriving, I find you
again: blue absence keeps knowledge alive,
makes of October an adjusted lens.
The days have almost no clouds left.

Cassiopeia, the Great Bear
let their signals burst by night
to rip into impossibility.
The Pleiades rage silently about.

To wait is the password; and to listen.
In Dwingelo you can hear it whisper,
the void in the radiotelescope.

There too the singing of your nerves is gathered,
becoming graphic on a sheet of paper
not unlike this one here.

THE DEMON LOVER

Fatigue, regrets. The lights
go out in the parking lot
two by two. Snow blindness
settles over the suburb.
Desire. Desire. The nebula
opens in space, unseen,
your heart utters its great beats
in solitude. A new
era is coming in.
Gauche as we are, it seems
we have to play our part.

A plaid dress, silk scarf,
and eyes that go on stinging.
Woman, stand off. The air
glistens like silk.
She's gone. In her place stands
a schoolgirl, morning light,
the half-grown bones
of innocence. Is she
your daughter or your muse,
this tree of blondness
grown up in a field of thorns?

Something piercing and marred.
Take note. Look back. When quick
the whole northeast went black
and prisoners howled and children
ran through the night with candles,
who stood off motionless
side by side while the moon swam up
over the drowned houses?
Who neither touched nor spoke?
whose nape, whose finger-ends
nervelessly lied the hours away?

A voice presses at me.
If I give in it won't
be like the girl the bull rode,
all Rubens flesh and happy moans.
But to be wrestled like a boy
with tongue, hips, knees, nerves, brain . . .
with language?
He doesn't know. He's watching
breasts under a striped blouse,
his bull's head down. The old
wine pours again through my veins.

Goodnight, then. 'Night. Again
we turn our backs and weary
weary we let down.
Things take us hard, no question.
How do you make it, all the way
from here to morning? I touch
you, made of such nerve
and flare and pride and swallowed tears.
Go home. Come to bed. The skies
look in at us, stern.
And this is an old story.

I dreamed about the war.
We were all sitting at table
in a kitchen in Chicago.
The radio had just screamed
that Illinois was the target.
No one felt like leaving,
we sat by the open window
and talked in the sunset.
I'll tell you that joke tomorrow,
you said with your saddest smile,
if I can remember.

The end is just a straw,
a feather furling slowly down,
floating to light by chance, a breath
on the long-loaded scales.
Posterity trembles like a leaf
and we go on making heirs and heirlooms.
The world, we have to make it,
my coexistent friend said, leaning
back in his cell.
Siberia vastly hulks
behind him, which he did not make.

Oh futile tenderness
of touch in a world like this!
how much longer, dear child,
do you think sex will matter?
There might have been a wedding
that never was:
two creatures sprung free
from castiron covenants.
Instead our hands and minds
erotically waver . . .
Lightness is unavailing.

Catalpas wave and spill
their dull strings across this murk of spring.
I ache, brilliantly.
Only where there is language is there world.
In the harp of my hair, compose me
a song. Death's in the air,
we all know that. Still, for an hour,
I'd like to be gay. How could a gay song go?
Why that's your secret, and it shall be mine.
We are our words, and black and bruised and blue.
Under our skins, we're laughing.

In triste veritas?
Take hold, sweet hands, come on . . .
Broken!
When you falter, all eludes.
This is a seasick way,
this almost/never touching, this
drawing-off, this to-and-fro.
Subtlety stalks in your eyes,
your tongue knows what it knows.
I want your secrets—I *will* have them out.
Seasick, I drop into the sea.

1966

❖ JERUSALEM

In my dream, children
are stoning other children
with blackened carob-pods
I dream my son is riding
on an old grey mare
to a half-dead war
on a dead-grey road
through the cactus and thistles
and dried brook-beds.

In my dream, children
are swaddled in smoke
and their uncut hair smolders
even here, here
where trees have no shade
and rocks have no shadow
trees have no memories
only the stones and
the hairs of the head.

I dream his hair is growing
and has never been shorn
from slender temples hanging
like curls of barbed wire
and his first beard is growing
smoldering like fire
his beard is smoke and fire
and I dream him riding
patiently to the war.

What I dream of the city
is how hard it is to leave
and how useless to walk
outside the blasted walls
picking up the shells

from a half-dead war
and I wake up in tears
and hear the sirens screaming
and the carob-tree is bare.

Balfour Street
July 1966

CHARLESTON IN THE 1860'S

Derived from the diaries of Mary Boykin Chesnut

He seized me by the waist and kissed my throat . . .
Your eyes, dear, are they grey or blue,
eyes of an angel?
The carts have passed already with their heaped
night-soil, we breathe again . . .
Is this what war is? Nitrate . . .
But smell the pear,
the jasmine, the violets.
Why does this landscape always sadden you?
Now the freshet is up on every side,
the river comes to our doors,
limbs of primeval trees dip in the swamp.

So we fool on into the black
cloud ahead of us.
Everything human glitters fever-bright—
the thrill of waking up
out of a stagnant life?
There seems a spell upon
your lovers, —all dead of wounds
or blown to pieces . . . Nitrate!
I'm writing, blind with tears of rage.
In vain. Years, death, depopulation, fears,
bondage—these shall all be borne.
No imagination to forestall woe.

1966

And now, outside, the walls
of black flint, eyeless.
How pale in sleep you lie.
Love: my love is just a breath
blown on the pane and dissolved.
Everything, even you,
cries silently for help, the web
of the spider is ripped with rain,
the geese fly on into the black cloud.
What can I do for you?
what can I do for you?
Can the touch of a finger mend
what a finger's touch has broken?
Blue-eyed now, yellow-haired,
I stand in my old nightmare
beside the track, while you,
and over and over and always you
plod into the deathcars.
Sometimes you smile at me
and I—I smile back at you.
How sweet the odor of the station-master's roses!
How pure, how poster-like the colors of this dream.

1967

◈ THERE ARE SUCH SPRINGLIKE NIGHTS
from the Yiddish of Kadia Maldovsky

There are such springlike nights here,
when a blade of grass pushes up through the soil
and the fresh dawn is a green pillow
under the skeleton of a dead horse.
And all the limbs of a woman plead for the ache of birth.
And women come to lie down like sick sheep
by the wells—to heal their bodies,
their faces blackened with yearlong thirst for a child's cry.

There are such springlike nights here
when lightning pierces the black soil with silver knives
and pregnant women approach the white tables of the hospital
with quiet steps
and smile at the unborn child
and perhaps at death.

There are such springlike nights here
when a blade of grass pushes up through the soil.

◈ FOR A RUSSIAN POET

1: *The winter dream.*

Everywhere, snow is falling. Your bandaged foot
drags across huge cobblestones, bells
hammer in distant squares.
Everything we stood against has conquered
and now we're part
of it all. *Life's the main thing,* I hear you say,
but a fog is spreading between this landmass
and the one your voice
mapped so long for me. All that's visible
is walls, endlessly yellow-grey, where
so many risks were taken, the shredded skies
slowly littering both our continents with
the only justice left, burying
footprints, bells and voices with all deliberate speed.

1967

2: *Summer in the country.*

Now, again, every year for years: the life-and-death talk,
late August, forebodings
under the birches, along the water's edge
and between the typed lines

and evenings, tracing a pattern of absurd hopes
in broken nutshells
                                    but this year we both
sit after dark with the radio
unable to read, unable to write

trying the blurred edges of broadcasts
for a little truth, taking a walk before bed
wondering what a man can do, asking that
at the verge of tears in a lightning-flash of loneliness.

3: *The demonstration.*

Natalya Gorbanevskaya
13/3 Novopeschanaya Street
Apartment 34

At noon we sit down quietly on the parapet
and unfurl our banners
                                almost immediately
the sound of police whistles
from all corners of Red Square
                                we sit
quietly and offer no resistance
Is this your little boy

we will relive this over and over

the banners torn
from our hands
                blood flowing
a great jagged torn place
in the silence of complicity

that much at least
we did here

In your flat, drinking tea
waiting for the police
your children asleep while you write
quickly, the letters you want to get off
before tomorrow

I'm a ghost at your table
touching poems in a script I can't read

we'll meet each other later

August 1968

◈NIGHT IN THE KITCHEN

The refrigerator falls silent.
Then other things are audible:
this dull, sheet-metal mind rattling like stage thunder.
The thickness budging forward in these veins
is surely something other
than blood:
say, molten lava.

You will become a black lace cliff fronting a deadpan sea;
nerves, friable as lightning
ending in burnt pine forests.
You are begun, beginning, your black heart drumming
slowly, triumphantly
inside its pacific cave.

1967

◈ 5:30 A.M.

Birds and periodic blood.
Old recapitulations.
The fox, panting, fire-eyed,
gone to earth in my chest.
How beautiful we are,
he and I, with our auburn
pelts, our trails of blood,
our miracle escapes,
our whiplash panic flogging us on
to new miracles!
They've supplied us with pills
for bleeding, pills for panic.
Wash them down the sink.
This is truth, then:
dull needle groping in the spinal fluid,
weak acid in the bottom of the cup,
foreboding, foreboding.
No one tells the truth about truth,
that it's what the fox
sees from his scuffled burrow:
dull-jawed, onrushing
killer, being that
inanely single-minded
will have our skins at last.

1967

◈ THE BREAK

All month eating the heart out,
smothering in a fierce insomnia . . .
First the long, spongy summer, drying
out by fits and starts, till a morning
torn off another calendar
when the wind stiffens, chairs
and tables rouse themselves
in a new, unplanned light
and a word flies like a dry leaf down the hall
at the bang of a door.

Then break, October, speak,
non-existent and damning clarity.
Stare me down, thrust
your tongue against mine, break
day, let me stand up
like a table or a chair
in a cold room with the sun beating in
full on the dusty panes.

1967

◈ TWO POEMS
adapted from Anna Akhmatova

1.

There's a secret boundary hidden in the waving grasses:
neither the lover nor the expert sensualist
passes it, though mouths press silently together
and the heart is bursting.

And friends—they too are helpless there,
and so with years of fire and joy,
whole histories of freedom
unburdened by sensual languor.

The crazy ones push on to that frontier
while those who have found it are sick with grief . . .
And now you know
why my heart doesn't beat beneath your hand.

2.

On the terrace, violins played
the most heartbreaking songs.
A sharp, fresh smell of the sea
came from oysters on a dish of ice

He said, *I'm a faithful friend,*
touching my dress.
How far from a caress,
the touch of that hand!

The way you stroke a cat, a bird,
the look you give a shapely bareback rider.
In his calm eyes, only laughter
under the light-gold lashes.

And the violins mourn on
behind drifting smoke:
Thank your stars, you're at last alone
with the man you love.

◇ THE KEY

Through a drain grating, something
    glitters and falters,
        glitters again. A scrap of foil,

a coin, a signal, a message
    from the indistinct
        piercing my indistinctness?

How long I have gone round
    and round, spiritless with foreknown defeat,
        in search of that glitter?

Hours, years maybe. The cry of metal
    on asphalt, on iron, the sudden
        ching of a precious loss,

the clear statement
    of something missing. Over and over
        it stops me in my tracks

like a falling star, only
    this is not the universe's loss
        it is mine. If I were only colder,

nearer death, nearer birth, I might let go
    whatever's so bent on staying lost.
        Why not leave the house

locked, to collapse inward among its weeds,
    the letters to darken and flake
        in the drawer, the car

to grow skeletal, aflame with rust
    in the moonlit lot, and walk
        ever after?

O God I am not spiritless,
    but a spirit can be stunned,
        a battery felt going dead

before the light flickers,
    and I've covered this ground too often
        with this yellow disc

within whose beam all's commonplace
    and whose limits are described
        by the whole night.

1967

◈ PICNIC

Sunday in Inwood Park
                  the picnic eaten
the chicken bones scattered
                    for the fox we'll never see
the children playing in the caves
My death is folded in my pocket
                      like a nylon raincoat
What kind of sunlight is it
                  that leaves the rocks so cold?

1967

◈ THE BOOK
for Richard Howard

You, hiding there in your words
like a disgrace
the cast-off son of a family
whose face is written in theirs
who must not be mentioned
who calls collect three times a year
from obscure towns out-of-state
and whose calls are never accepted
You who had to leave alone
and forgot your shadow hanging under the stairs
let me tell you: I have been in the house
I have spoken to all of them
they will not pronounce your name
they only allude to you
rising and sitting, going or coming,
falling asleep and waking,
giving away in marriage or calling for water
on their deathbeds
their faces look into each other and see
you
when they write at night in their diaries they are writing
to you

1968

◆ ABNEGATION

The red fox, the vixen
dancing in the half-light among the junipers,
wise-looking in a sexy way,
Egyptian-supple in her sharpness—
what does she want
with the dreams of dead vixens,
the apotheosis of Reynard,
the literature of fox-hunting?
Only in her nerves the past
sings, a thrill of self-preservation.
I go along down the road
to a house nailed together by Scottish
Covenanters, instinct mortified
in a virgin forest,
and she springs toward her den
every hair on her pelt alive
with tidings of the immaculate present.
They left me a westernness,
a birthright, a redstained, ravelled
afghan of sky.
She has no archives,
no heirlooms, no future
except death
and I could be more
her sister than theirs
who chopped their way across these hills
—a chosen people.

1968

◈
PART TWO
◈
LEAFLETS

◈ WOMEN
   for C.R.G.

My three sisters are sitting
on rocks of black obsidian.
For the first time, in this light, I can see who they are.

My first sister is sewing her costume for the procession.
She is going as the Transparent Lady
and all her nerves will be visible.

My second sister is also sewing,
at the seam over her heart which has never healed entirely.
At last, she hopes, this tightness in her chest will ease.

My third sister is gazing
at a dark-red crust spreading westward far out on the sea.
Her stockings are torn but she is beautiful.

1968

◈ IMPLOSIONS

The world's
not wanton
only wild and wavering

I wanted to choose words that even you
would have to be changed by

Take the word
of my pulse, loving and ordinary
Send out your signals, hoist
your dark scribbled flags
but take
my hand

All wars are useless to the dead

My hands are knotted in the rope
and I cannot sound the bell

My hands are frozen to the switch
and I cannot throw it

The foot is in the wheel

When it's finished and we're lying
in a stubble of blistered flowers
eyes gaping, mouths staring
dusted with crushed arterial blues

I'll have done nothing
even for you?

1968

◈ TO FRANTZ FANON

born Martinique, 1925; dead Washington D.C.,
1961

I don't see your head
sunk, listening   to the throats
of the torturers and the tortured

I don't see your eyes
deep in the blackness   of your skull
they look off from me   into the eyes

of rats and haunted policemen.
What I see best is the length
of your fingers
pressing the pencil
into the barred page

of the French child's-copybook
with its Cartesian squares   its grilled
trap of holy geometry
where your night-sweats streamed out
in language

and your death
a black streak on a white bed
in L'Enfant's city where
the fever-bush sweats off
its thick
petals   year after year
on the mass grave
of revolt

1968

◈ CONTINUUM

Waking thickheaded by crow's light
I see the suitcase packed
for your early plane; nothing to do
but follow the wristwatch hands
round to the hour. Life is like money
—you said, finishing the brandy from the cracked
plastic bathroom cup last night—
no use except for what you can get with it.
Yet something wants us delivered up
alive, whatever it is,
that causes me to edge the slatted blind
soundlessly up, leaving you
ten minutes' more sleep, while I look
shivering, lucidifying, down
at that street where the poor are already getting started
and that poster streaking the opposite wall
with the blurred face of a singer whose songs
money can't buy nor air contain
someone yet unloved, whose voice
I may never hear, but go on hoping
to hear, tonight, tomorrow, someday,
as I go on hoping to feel
tears of mercy in the of course impersonal rain.

1968

◈ ON EDGES

When the ice starts to shiver
all across the reflecting basin
or water-lily leaves
dissect a simple surface
the word 'drowning' flows through me.
You built a glassy floor
that held me
as I leaned to fish for old
hooks and toothed tin cans,
stems lashing out like ties of
silk dressing-gowns
archangels of lake-light
gripped in mud.

Now you hand me a torn letter.
On my knees, in the ashes, I could never
fit these ripped-up flakes together.
In the taxi I am still piecing
what syllables I can
translating at top speed like a thinking machine
that types out 'useless' as 'monster'
and 'history' as 'lampshade'.
Crossing the bridge I need all my nerve
to trust to the man-made cables.

The blades on that machine
could cut you to ribbons
but its function is humane.
Is this all I can say of these
delicate hooks, scythe-curved intentions
you and I handle? I'd rather
taste blood, yours or mine, flowing
from a sudden slash, than cut all day
with blunt scissors on dotted lines
like the teacher told.

1968

◈ VIOLENCE

No one knows yet
what he is capable of. Thus: if you
(still drawing me, mouth to mouth
toward the door) had pushed
a gun into my hand
would my fingers have burned, or not,
to dry ice on that metal?
if you'd said, leaving
in a pre-dawn thunderstorm
use this when the time comes
would I have blurted
my first *no* that night
or, back without you, bundled
the cold bulk into a drawer
in a cocoon of nightgowns
printed with knots of honeysuckle . . .
Still following you as if your body
were a lantern, an angel of radar,
along the untrustworthy park
or down that block where the cops shoot to kill—
could I have dreamed a violence
like that of finding
your burnt-out cigarettes
planted at random, charred
fuses in a blown-up field?

1968

◈ THE OBSERVER

Completely protected on all sides
by volcanoes
a woman, darkhaired, in stained jeans
sleeps in central Africa.
In her dreams, her notebooks, still
private as maiden diaries,
the mountain gorillas move through their life term;
their gentleness survives
observation. Six bands of them
inhabit, with her, the wooded highland.
When I lay me down to sleep
unsheltered by any natural guardians
from the panicky life-cycle of my tribe
I wake in the old cellblock
observing the daily executions,
rehearsing the laws
I cannot subscribe to,
envying the pale gorilla-scented dawn
she wakes into, the stream where she washes her hair,
the camera-flash of her quiet
eye.

1968

◆ NIGHTBREAK

Something broken   Something
I need   By someone
I love   Next year
will I remember what
This anger   unreal
                     yet
has to be gone through
The sun to set
on this anger
              I go on
head down   into it
The mountain pulsing
Into the oildrum   drops
the ball of fire.

Time is quiet   doesn't break things
or even wound   Things are in danger
from people   The frail clay lamps
of Mesopotamia
row on row under glass
in the ethnological section
little hollows for dried-
up oil   The refugees
with their identical
tales of escape   I don't
collect what I can't use   I need
what can be broken.

In the bed the pieces fly together
and the rifts fill   or else
my body is a list   of wounds
symmetrically placed
a village
blown open   by planes
that did not   finish the job

The enemy has   withdrawn
between raids   become invisible
there are
          no agencies
               of relief
the darkness becomes utter
Sleep   cracked and flaking
sifts over the shaken   target

What breaks   is night
not day   The white
scar   splitting
over the east
The crack weeping
Time for the pieces
          to move
dumbly back
          toward each other.

1968

49

❖ GABRIEL

There are no angels   yet
here comes an angel   one
with a man's face   young
shut-off   the dark
side of the moon   turning to me
and saying: I am the plumed
            serpent   the beast
            with fangs of fire   and a gentle
            heart

But he doesn't say that   His message
drenches his body
he'd want to kill me
for using words to name him

I sit in the bare apartment
reading
words stream past me   poetry
twentieth-century rivers
disturbed surfaces   reflecting clouds
reflecting wrinkled neon
but clogged   and mostly
nothing alive left
in their depths

The angel is barely
speaking   to me
Once in a horn of light
he stood   or someone like him
salutations in gold-leaf
ribboning from his lips
Today again   the hair streams
to his shoulders
the eyes reflect   something
like a lost country   or so I think

but the ribbon has reeled itself
up
    he isn't giving
or taking any shit
We glance miserably
across the room   at each other

It's true   there are moments
closer and closer together
when words stick   in my throat
                  the art of love'
                  'the art of words'
I get your message Gabriel
just   will you stay looking
straight at me
awhile longer

1968

LEAFLETS

1.

The big star, and that other
lonely on black glass
overgrown with frozen
lesions, endless night
the Coal Sack gaping
black veins of ice on the pane
spelling a word:
                    Insomnia
not manic but ordinary
to start out of sleep
turning off and on
this seasick neon
vision, this
division

the head clears of sweet smoke
and poison gas

life without caution
the only worth living
love for a man
love for a woman
love for the facts
protectless

that self-defense be not
the arm's first motion

memory not only
cards of identity

that I can live half a year
as I have never lived up to this time—

Chekhov coughing up blood almost daily
the steamer edging in toward the penal colony
chained men dozing on deck
five forest fires lighting the island

lifelong that glare, waiting.

2.

Your face
            stretched like a mask
                        begins to tear
as you speak of Che Guevara
Bolivia, Nanterre
I'm too young to be your mother
you're too young to be my brother

your tears are not political
they are real water, burning
as the tears of Telemachus
burned

Over Spanish Harlem the moon
swells up, a fire balloon
fire gnawing the edge
of this crushed-up newspaper

                                    now
the bodies come whirling
coal-black, ash-white
out of torn windows
and the death columns blacken
                        whispering
Who'd choose this life?

We're fighting for a slash of recognition,
a piercing to the pierced heart.
Tell me what you are going through—

but the attention flickers
                    and will flicker
a matchflame in poison air
a thread, a hair of light
                    sum of all answer
to the *Know that I exist!* of all existing things.

3.

If, says the Dahomeyan devil,
someone has courage to enter the fire
the young man will be restored to life.

If, the girl whispers,
I do not go into the fire
I will not be able to live with my soul.

(Her face calm and dark as amber
under the dyed butterfly turban
her back scarified in ostrich-skin patterns.)

4.

Crusaders' wind glinting
off linked scales of sea
ripping the ghostflags
galloping at the fortress
Acre, bloodcaked, lionhearted
raw vomit curdling in the sun
gray walkers walking
straying with a curbed intentness

in and out the inclosures
the gallows, the photographs
of dead Jewish terrorists, aged 15
their fading faces wide-eyed
and out in the crusading sunlight
gray strayers still straying
dusty paths
the mad who live in the dried-up moat
of the War Museum

what are we coming to
what wants these things of us
who wants them

5.

The strain of being born
     over and over has torn your smile into pieces
Often I have seen it broken
     and then re-membered
and wondered how a beauty
     so anarch, so ungelded
will be cared for in this world.
     I want to hand you this
leaflet streaming with rain or tears
     but the words coming clear
something you might find crushed into your hand
     after passing a barricade
and stuff in your raincoat pocket.
     I want this to reach you
who told me once that poetry is nothing sacred
     —no more sacred that is
than other things in your life—
     to answer yes, if life is uncorrupted
no better poetry is wanted.

I want this to be yours
in the sense that if you find and read it
    it will be there in you already
and the leaflet then merely something
    to leave behind, a little leaf
in the drawer of a sublet room.
    What else does it come down to
but handing on scraps of paper
    little figurines or phials
no stronger than the dry clay they are baked in
    yet more than dry clay or paper
because the imagination crouches in them.
    If we needed fire to remind us
that all true images
    were scooped out of the mud
where our bodies curse and flounder
    then perhaps that fire is coming
to sponge away the scribes and time-servers
    and much that you would have loved will be lost as well
before you could handle it and know it
    just as we almost miss each other
in the ill cloud of mistrust, who might have touched
    hands quickly, shared food or given blood
for each other. I am thinking how we can use what we have
    to invent what we need.

Winter–Spring 1968

◈ THE RAFTS
for David, Michael and David

Down the river, on rafts you came
floating. The three of you
and others I can't remember.
Stuck to your sleeves, twists of
blurred red rag, old bandages, ribbons
of honor.   Your hands dragged me
aboard.

      Then I sprawled
full length on the lashed poles
laughing, drenched, in rags.

The river's rising!

              they yelled on shore
thru megaphones.
Can't you see
that water's mad, those rafts
are children's toys, that crowd
is heading nowhere?

           My lips
tasted your lips and foreheads
salty with sweat,
then we were laughing, holding off
the scourge of dead branches
overhanging from shore as your
homemade inventions

                danced

                   along

1968

PART THREE

GHAZALS:

HOMAGE TO GHALIB

This poem began to be written after I read Aijaz Ahmad's literal English versions of the work of the Urdu poet Mirza Ghalib, 1797–1869. While the structure and metrics used by Ghalib are much stricter than mine, I have adhered to his use of a minimum five couplets to a *ghazal*, each couplet being autonomous and independent of the others. The continuity and unity flow from the associations and images playing back and forth among the couplets in any single *ghazal*.

My *ghazals* are personal and public, American and twentieth-century; but they owe much to the presence of Ghalib in my mind: a poet self-educated and profoundly learned, who owned no property and borrowed his books, writing in an age of political and cultural break-up.

I have left the *ghazals* dated as I wrote them.

◈ GHAZALS: HOMAGE TO GHALIB
7/12/68
for Sheila Rotner

The clouds are electric in this university.
The lovers astride the tractor burn fissures through the hay.

When I look at that wall I shall think of you
and of what you did not paint there.

Only the truth makes the pain of lifting a hand worthwhile:
the prism staggering under the blows of the raga.

The vanishing-point is the point where he appears.
Two parallel tracks converge, yet there has been no wreck.

To mutilate privacy with a single foolish syllable
is to throw away the search for the one necessary word.

When you read these lines, think of me
and of what I have not written here.

7/13/68

The ones who camped on the slopes, below the bare summit,
saw differently from us, who breathed thin air and kept walking.

Sleeping back-to-back, man and woman, we were more conscious
than either of us awake and alone in the world.

These words are vapor-trails of a plane that has vanished;
by the time I write them out, they are whispering something else.

Do we still have to feel jealous of our creations?
Once they might have outlived us; in this world, we'll die together.

Don't look for me in the room I have left;
the photograph shows just a white rocking-chair, still rocking.

7/14/68: i

In Central Park we talked of our own cowardice.
How many times a day, in this city, are those words spoken?

The tears of the universe aren't all stars, Danton;
some are satellites of brushed aluminum and stainless steel.

He, who was temporary, has joined eternity;
he has deserted us, gone over to the other side.

In the Theatre of the Dust no actor becomes famous.
In the last scene they all are blown away like dust.

"It may be if I had known them I would have loved them."
You were American, Whitman, and those words are yours.

7/14/68: ii

Did you think I was talking about my life?
I was trying to drive a tradition up against the wall.

The field they burned over is greener than all the rest.
You have to watch it, he said, the sparks can travel the roots.

Shot back into this earth's atmosphere
our children's children may photograph these stones.

In the red wash of the darkroom, I see myself clearly;
when the print is developed and handed about, the face is nothing to
                                                       me.

For us the work undoes itself over and over:
the grass grows back, the dust collects, the scar breaks open.

7/16/68: i

Blacked-out on a wagon, part of my life cut out forever—
five green hours and forty violet minutes.

A cold spring slowed our lilacs, till a surf broke
violet/white, tender and sensual, misread it if you dare.

I tell you, truth is, at the moment, here
burning outward through our skins.

Eternity streams through my body:
touch it with your hand and see.

Till the walls of the tunnel cave in
and the black river walks on our faces.

7/16/68: ii

When they mow the fields, I see the world reformed
as if by snow, or fire, or physical desire.

First snow. Death of the city. Ghosts in the air.
Your shade among the shadows, interviewing the mist.

The mail came every day, but letters were missing;
by this I knew things were not what they ought to be.

The trees in the long park blurring back
into Olmstead's original dream-work.

The impartial scholar writes me from under house arrest.
I hope you are rotting in hell, Montaigne you bastard.

7/17/68

Armitage of scrapiron for the radiations of a moon.
Flower cast in metal, Picasso-woman, sister.

Two hesitant Luna moths regard each other
with the spots on their wings: fascinated.

To resign *yourself*—what an act of betrayal!
—to throw a runaway spirit back to the dogs.

When the ebb-tide pulls hard enough, we are all starfish.
The moon has her way with us, my companion in crime.

At the Aquarium that day, between the white whale's loneliness
and the groupers' mass promiscuities, only ourselves.

7/23/68

When your sperm enters me, it is altered;
when my thought absorbs yours, a world begins.

If the mind of the teacher is not in love with the mind of the student,
he is simply practising rape, and deserves at best our pity.

To live outside the law! Or, barely within it,
a twig on boiling waters, enclosed inside a bubble.

Our words are jammed in an electronic jungle;
sometimes, though, they rise and wheel croaking above the treetops.

An open window; thick summer night; electric fences trilling.
What are you doing here at the edge of the death-camps, Vivaldi?

7/24/68: i

The sapling springs, the milkweed blooms: obsolete Nature.
In the woods I have a vision of asphalt, blindly lingering.

I hardly know the names of the weeds I love.
I have forgotten the names of so many flowers.

I can't live at the hems of that tradition—
will I last to try the beginning of the next?

Killing is different now: no fingers round the throat.
No one feels the wetness of the blood on his hands.

When we fuck, there too are we remoter
than the fucking bodies of lovers used to be?

How many men have touched me with their eyes
more hotly than they later touched me with their lips.

7/24/68: **ii**

The friend I can trust is the one who will let me have my death.
The rest are actors who want me to stay and further the plot.

At the drive-in movie, above the PanaVision,
beyond the projector beams, you project yourself, great Star.

The eye that used to watch us is dead, but open.
Sometimes I still have a sense of being followed.

How long will we be waiting for the police?
How long must I wonder which of my friends would hide me?

Driving at night I feel the Milky Way
streaming above me like the graph of a cry.

7/26/68: i

Last night you wrote on the wall: Revolution is poetry.
Today you needn't write; the wall has tumbled down.

We were taught to respect the appearance behind the reality.
Our senses were out on parole, under surveillance.

A pair of eyes imprisoned for years inside my skull
is burning its way outward, the headaches are terrible.

I'm walking through a rubble of broken sculpture, stumbling
here on the spine of a friend, there on the hand of a brother.

All those joinings! and yet we fought so hard to be unique.
Neither alone, nor in anyone's arms, will we end up sleeping.

7/26/68: ii

A dead mosquito, flattened against a door;
his image could survive our comings and our goings.

LeRoi! Eldridge! listen to us, we are ghosts
condemned to haunt the cities where you want to be at home.

The white children turn black on the negative.
The summer clouds blacken inside the camera-skull.

Every mistake that can be made, we are prepared to make;
anything less would fall short of the reality we're dreaming.

Someone has always been desperate, now it's our turn—
we who were free to weep for Othello and laugh at Caliban.

I have learned to smell a *conservateur* a mile away:
they carry illustrated catalogues of all that there is to lose.

7/26/68: iii

So many minds in search of bodies
groping their way among artificial limbs.

Of late they write me how they are getting on:
desertion, desertion, is the story of those pages.

A chewed-up nail, the past, splitting yet growing,
the same and not the same; a nervous habit never shaken.

Those stays of tooled whalebone in the Salem museum—
erotic scrimshaw, practical even in lust.

Whoever thought of inserting a ship in a bottle?
Long weeks without women do this to a man.

8/1/68

The order of the small town on the riverbank,
forever at war with the order of the dark and starlit soul.

Were you free then all along, Jim, free at last,
of everything but the white boy's fantasies?

We pleaded guilty till we saw what rectitude was like:
its washed hands, and dead nerve, and sclerotic eye.

I long ago stopped dreaming of pure justice, your honor—
my crime was to believe we could make cruelty obsolete.

The body has been exhumed from the burnt-out bunker;
the teeth counted, the contents of the stomach told over.

And you, Custer, the Squaw-killer, hero of primitive schoolrooms—
where are you buried, what is the condition of your bones?

8/4/68

for Aijaz Ahmad

If these are letters, they will have to be misread.
If scribblings on a wall, they must tangle with all the others.

Fuck reds   Black Power   Angel loves Rosita
—and a transistor radio answers in Spanish: *Night must fall.*

Prisoners, soldiers, crouching as always, writing,
explaining the unforgivable to a wife, a mother, a lover.

Those faces are blurred and some have turned away
to which I used to address myself so hotly.

How is it, Ghalib, that your grief, resurrected in pieces,
has found its way to this room from your dark house in Delhi?

When they read this poem of mine, they are translators.
Every existence speaks a language of its own.

8/8/68: i

From here on, all of us will be living
like Galileo turning his first tube at the stars.

Obey the little laws and break the great ones
is the preamble to their constitution.

Even to hope is to leap into the unknown,
under the mocking eyes of the way things are.

There's a war on earth, and in the skull, and in the glassy spaces,
between the existing and the non-existing.

I need to live each day through, have them and know them all,
though I can see from here where I'll be standing at the end.

8/8/68: ii
for A.H.C.

A piece of thread ripped-out from a fierce design,
some weaving figured as magic against oppression.

I'm speaking to you as a woman to a man:
when your blood flows I want to hold you in my arms.

How did we get caught up fighting this forest fire,
we, who were only looking for a still place in the woods?

How frail we are, and yet, dispersed, always returning,
the barnacles they keep scraping from the warship's hull.

The hairs on your breast curl so lightly as you lie there,
while the strong heart goes on pounding in its sleep.

◈

NOTES ON THE POEMS:

The Dutch poems in this book are translations, in the sense that they were derived by me directly from their originals. The Russian poems are adaptations of literal prose versions in the *Penguin Book of Russian Verse*, and will appear in *Poets on Street Corners*, an anthology of Russian poetry edited by Olga Carlisle, to be published by Random House in 1969. The Yiddish poem is, similarly, an adaptation from a literal version furnished by Eliezer Greenberg and Irving Howe, and will be included in their forthcoming anthology of Yiddish poetry in translation. It appears here with their permission and that of Kadia Maldovsky.

Orion. One or two phrases suggested by Gottfried Benn's essay 'Artists and Old Age' in *Primal Vision*, edited by E. B. Ashton. (New Directions)

Dwingelo. The site of an astronomical observatory in Holland.

Charleston in the 1860's. See *A Diary from Dixie*, edited by Ben Ames Williams. (Houghton Mifflin)

Implosions. The first three lines are stolen, by permission, from Abbott Small.

To Frantz Fanon. Psychiatrist and revolutionary philosopher; studied medicine at the Sorbonne; worked as psychiatrist in Algeria during the Franco-Algerian war; died of cancer at the age of 36.

The Observer. Derived from a brief newspaper account of the field-work of an associate of Dr. L. S. B. Leakey.

Leaflets. (Section 3) Simone Weil: 'The love of a fellow-creature in all its fullness consists simply in the ability to say to him: "What are you going through?" '—*Waiting For God.*

The Demonstration. Derived from an account by Natalya Gorbanevskaya, poet, of a protest action in Moscow against the invasion of Czechoslovakia.